DELICIOUS BIBLE STORIES

No-Cook Recipes That Teach

Daphna Flegal
LeeDell Stickler

Delicious Bible Stories

ISBN: 978-1-4267-0032-3
PACP00456924-02

Writers: Daphna Flegal and LeeDell Stickler
Cover and interior design and photos: Paige Easter

10 11 12 13 14 15 16 17 18—10 9 8 7 6 5 4 3 2

Contents

Introduction

The Event

Delicious Bible Stories is a participatory event. The presentation takes approximately one and a half hours. The preparation for the event takes a bit more time. The more participants you have, the more time it will take to prepare and present. Also, the younger the participants, the longer it will take. Don't rush the event. Give the participants time to reflect and enjoy the experience.

There is more than one way to present this material. On pages 15–17, we provide several alternative presentations. Some of these were recommended to us the first few times we presented *Delicious Bible Stories*. Adapt this event to whatever situation and space allocation you have.

Preparation Time

Delicious Bible Stories requires significant preparation. (But then, what worthwhile endeavor doesn't?) You cannot walk into the room with this book and do it with very much success. It takes careful planning and pre-presentation work.

Part of the fun of the event is the "getting it together." Plan a work day with the volunteers the day before the event. We have done the research and have organized the material for you. Use the checklists to make sure everything is done.

Age and Number of Participants

Delicious Bible Stories can be done as an event for children ages five to twelve. Preschool children are usually unable to sustain interest for the entire presentation. But that doesn't mean they won't benefit from the stories and the foods. Divide *Delicious Bible Stories* into five smaller events for the younger ones. *Delicious Bible Stories* is also interesting and fun for youth and adults, so an intergenerational group is also a possibility.

4

Caution: In an intergenerational experience, do not have all children at a table together. Mix it up to control the chaos.

Delicious Bible Stories can be done as a "tasting," where leaders provide the participants with pre-prepared foods. But in order to fully appreciate the cuisine and culture of Bible times, you will want to provide an opportunity for the participants to be part of the preparation as well. In this more-expanded version, each table group will prepare a small amount of a particular food for that table. It creates fun, promotes teamwork, and provides a sense of what life might have been like for the women who prepared the food in those times. (Men were rarely involved in preparation.)

Space and Seating

You will need a rather large space to present *Delicious Bible Stories*. A fellowship hall or large social room provides the ideal setting. See "Front Stage Layout" on page 23. A larger room also indicates the need for microphones. You will need two.

If you need to present the event in a "lecture style" setup, refer to those instructions on the top of page 16. If you plan to do the event around tables, you will need tables that will accommodate at least six people. Adjust the recipes accordingly. Most of the recipes allow for just a "taste" of the foods. If you intend for *Delicious Bible Stories* to be a full-blown meal, expand the final dish (Rooster Tabbouleh Salad With Mint). You will need serving assistance at that point.

Helpful Hint: Pre-measure all the ingredients. The first time we presented *Delicious Bible Stories*, to save time, we simply set ingredients on the tables. The participants assumed if it was in a container and on the table, it went into the mixture—all of it. We had some strange tasting foods that time.

5

Overview

Welcome to *Delicious Bible Stories*, an event that will change the way you look at Bible stories forever. This is not a book you sit down with and read. This is a book that helps you plan a unique experience with five Bible stories and gives participants a renewed appreciation of the role that food preparation and the act of eating had in everyday life in Bible times.

One of the most common complaints about Bible stories is that they are hard to understand. The Bible tells real stories about real people engaged in real life. But the world view that existed at the time of the stories is one we have difficulty relating to. That's where *Delicious Bible Stories* comes in. If we can find ways to make this culture and this life more meaningful, then it seems to reason that the stories from this time and this culture will come to life. *Delicious Bible Stories* will guide you through the planning and the presentation of a special event, one that the participants will remember for a long time.

The Bible is filled with references to food and to meals. Food was the center of the social life of the Hebrew people. In fact, one of the very first stories in the Bible shows what happens when someone takes a single bite of something that he shouldn't have eaten.

Food and the Bible are inseparably linked. Eating and drinking together among the people of the Bible was more than simply an act of nourishing the body. Sometimes, eating together signified a bond of friendship that was highly respected. Sometimes, a meal was the agreement to a contract, such as Esau's signing away his birthright. Sometimes, food became a metaphor, such as in the parable of the sower. Regardless, food was more than food, and in this book you'll discover just how important it was. The event is set out as a "cooking/variety show" on television. Our hostess, Rebekah Ray, welcomes five special guests.

These guests not only dress the part and share their Bible stories, but they also share their authentic recipes. Participants at the table will then prepare each recipe and sample it as they hear the story.

Story 1: Abraham and Sarah
(Genesis 18:1-15; 21:1-7)

Delicious Bible Stories begins with a story from the saga of the patriarch Abraham and his wife, Sarah. The story is told from the point of view of one of Sarah's servants, who would have helped prepare the foods they ate. This story tells about the time when three men stopped by Abraham's tents and reminded Abraham that God intended to fulfill the promise that God had made many years earlier. Sarah, now at an advanced age, found it hard to believe. But she would "eat her words" one year later.

Story 2: Abigail and David
(1 Samuel 25:2-42)

In this story, we hear how Nabal, a local sheep farmer, refused to offer hospitality to David and his men. Hospitality was something that was expected rather than hoped for, and Nabal's refusal started a series of potentially serious events. Abigail, Nabal's wife, realized what a mistake Nabal had made and quickly moved to rectify the situation. The story is told from the point of view of Abigail, who overstepped the wishes of her husband and prevented a war.

Story 3: Queen Esther
(Book of Esther)

The story of Esther's great courage is told every year at the Jewish Festival of Purim. It is a story filled with action, intrigue, humor, irony, suspense, and, of course, love. The story is set after the fall of Jerusalem in 587 B.C., when God's people were living in exile in Persia and discovering who they were as God's people in a foreign land. Queen Esther relates her story and gives us a little insight into life at the palace.

Story 4: A Wedding at Cana
(John 2:1-11)

Everybody loves a wedding, and this was equally true in Bible times as it is today. It was at the wedding festival that Jesus first revealed himself to his friends as the promised one from God. This was only the first among many of his signs and miracles. This story is told from the point of view of one of the bridesmaids, who would have attended the festivities.

Story 5: Caiaphas' Courtyard
(Luke 22:54-62)

Judas led the Temple guards to the garden where Jesus and his friends were keeping watch and praying. Jesus was arrested there and led away to the high priest's house. His friends fled. He was all alone, facing a council that was not very happy with what he was teaching. To Peter's credit, however, Peter followed behind even though he was too scared to take a stand. Hiding in the shadows, he tried to discover what was happening to his friend and teacher. When the rooster crowed at dawn, Peter remembered what Jesus had said to him only a few hours earlier at the Passover meal: "Peter, before the rooster crows, you will say three times that you do not know me." How right he was. This story is told from the point of view of the servant girl who recognized Peter and showed that words were easy and actions much tougher.

GETTING STARTED

A Bible Times Food Primer

A Healthy Cuisine

The cuisine of the Bible was a healthy one. All the bread and grain dishes were whole grain. Beans and raw vegetables were eaten frequently, as were yogurt and simple cheeses. Poultry and fish were more common than meat, which was usually reserved for special occasions or special guests. Besides, when a lamb or a calf or a goat was sacrificed for a meal, the herd was diminished. Since there was little means of preservation, foods needed to be eaten at once. No one wanted any foods to go to waste. Fruits and nuts were the main ingredients in the sauces and desserts. Refined sugar didn't exist, and sweeteners were usually made from dates, grapes, and the old standby, honey.

A Wide Variety of Foods

Because Palestine was a "land bridge" between powerful armies, the culture suffered radical changes from time to time as armies marched through the land. The people of God were influenced by the Egyptians to the west, Persia to the east, Turkey and Greece to the north, and Africa to the south.

The earliest people were nomadic. They didn't stay in one place long enough to cultivate crops year after year after year. They hunted animals that were nearby and learned to recognize and use wild herbs and other seasonings. Because there were no grocery stores, no restaurants, and no means of preservation, most of the foods that were consumed were eaten fresh (with the exception of dried fruits, olives pickled in a strong brine, and parched grains).

Significance of Eating

Eating and drinking together among the people of Bible lands signified a bond of friendship, even if they had never met before the meal. To share food was to forget all past grievances. This made the act of eating almost a sacred affair.

10

In keeping with this tradition, the Hebrew people were also forbidden to eat with the Gentiles. To do so would cause uncleanness. In fact, one of God's people could not even touch a Gentile or anything that had been handled by a Gentile.

Bread of Life

Jesus frequently referred to himself as the "bread of life" (John 6:48). In Bible times, bread was a staple food. The term "breaking bread" came to mean sharing a meal with others. Think about the number of times Jesus "broke bread" with his friends and even with the outcasts of society. At one gathering Jesus even provided bread for a crowd of five thousand men (and a few more women and children) who had come to hear him preach. When he did these things, surely the crowd remembered the story of God providing bread for the Hebrew people in the wilderness. The promised Messiah would provide bread again.

Bread was made from a variety of grains, depending upon the availability. Wheat was a primary grain crop, but it was difficult to grow and was cultivated mostly in the coastal plains and near the Jordan Valley, where water was plentiful.

Barley wasn't as fussy as oats or wheat. It was hardier and could be grown most anywhere. Its durability in the heat made it a dependable crop. Bread made from barley was coarse and dark in color. Barley was the food of the poor.

Eat Your Vegetables

Vegetables were not regarded by the children of Bible times as they are today. Sometimes, vegetables were the only food available. Dried beans were used during the winter for savory vegetable stews and were a staple of the Bible-times diet. You would probably recognize some of the beans they used: fava beans, garbanzo beans, and a bean similar to a lima bean.

Beans were allowed to dry on the plant and were often crushed and added to grain to make a coarse bread. This might not have been particularly appetizing, but it was great fiber. Obviously, beans were a staple in the diet of the poor.

Another vegetable that showed up on the Bible-times table was the cucumber. There were two main varieties. One was long, dark, and slender. The other was smaller, whitish, and smooth-skinned. The Hebrews used to build towers in their gardens so that the cucumber would have ample room to grow.

Garlic and onions were also a part of the diet in Palestine. They grew well in the hot climate and provided a tasty flavor to the vegetable stews and meat dishes. Garlic and onions were a basic in their diet while they lived in Egypt. In the story of the Exodus, these were two vegetables the Hebrew people particularly missed while in the wilderness.

Grapes and Figs and Dates, Oh My!

Fruits were a welcome seasonal addition to the normal diet of the people of Bible times. There were grapes, figs, dates, pomegranates, olives, and a variety of citrus fruits (mostly in New Testament times). The fruits people couldn't eat while they were in season were dried and stored for use later in the year.

Grapes, raisins, and wine are mentioned frequently in the Bible. The climate in Palestine was perfect for growing grapes. But not everyone had a vineyard. Many people were too poor to be able to purchase fresh grapes from the market. But the poor were always considered. The grape pickers were allowed to go through the vineyard only one time. Any grapes that were left belonged to the poor who came behind them. No one in the community was left out.

The fig tree was a welcome addition to the garden or courtyard in Bible times. Every homeowner dreamed of having a fig tree, not only for the wonderful fruit but also for the shade the large fig tree leaves provided in the heat of the summer. Figs were picked as soon as they were ripe, because they were highly perishable. Any fig that was not eaten within a few days was immediately dried. Cities kept stores of dried figs available, just in case an enemy lay siege to their city.

One of the recipes included in this book substitutes dates for figs. Figs in the United States tend to be expensive, but dates are more readily available. Even though dates are not mentioned in the Bible, they were certainly eaten, both fresh and dried. Dates could even be boiled down to produce a sticky sweetener similar to honey.

Also available were pomegranates and a variety of citrus fruits. Citrus such as lemons, limes, and oranges were a luxury and were not cultivated until later times. But the citron was common, even during Old Testament times. The citron, however, was almost more work that it was worth, as the peel could be very thick and the juice sparse.

Olives were the most important crop in all of Palestine. They grew on trees and could be eaten fresh during the harvest in the fall. Some were pickled in a strong salt brine. But most were pressed for the oil that could be gotten from them.

The Fatted Calf, Etc.

Meat was a rare occurrence at a meal unless it was a festival or a very special occasion. Most meats were boiled or stewed with the vegetables. During Passover, however, the lamb was roasted over a fire. Mutton was more common than beef. Because of lack of refrigeration, it had to be a very special occasion to "kill the fatted calf." Fish, on the other hand was accessible to most of the people, even the poor. In fact, fish was a part of most everyday meals. Those who did not live close to water preserved fish through drying, pickling, or salting. Jesus' first followers were men who made a living in the fishing industry.

13

Grocery List for the Event

✓ | ITEMS NEEDED

canned chickpeas
tahini (sesame paste)
plain yogurt
honey
lemon juice
salt
olive oil
dried pitted dates
chopped walnuts
chopped almonds
canned hearts of palm
cream cheese (softened)
2½–3 cups diced
    grilled chicken
fine bulgur wheat
red or yellow pepper

plum tomatoes
green onions
romaine lettuce leaves
minced garlic
ground cumin
paprika
parsley (flakes)
ground cinnamon
ground cardamom
dill
coriander
black cumin seed
mint (fresh or flakes)
ground pepper
horseradish
pita bread

NOTE: Amounts of each item are not specifically listed. You will need to determine how much of each item you need after you discover how many people will be participating in the event and which model you plan to use.

How to Do Delicious Bible Stories

The good thing about *Delicious Bible Stories* is that there is not just one way to do the event. We have done it all three ways and have learned from each one. There are pluses and minuses with each. We have even had suggestions of ways to break the event down into bite-sized chunks that can be used during Lenten studies or on Sunday mornings or Sunday evenings. The basics for this event are all here: the recipes for the foods, the story scripts, and the setup information. How you choose to do it is up to you.

Model #1: One-Time Event Around Tables

Time: 1½ hours

Script: A (see pages 26–42)

Presenters: 2–7; 1 hostess, 1 announcer, and 1–5 storytellers (One storyteller can change costumes, be the announcer, and tell all 5 stories. Or you may use 5 storytellers and 1 announcer.)

Number of participants: As many as the space holds

Plus: Active participation

Minus: A great deal of pre-event preparation

The first three times we did *Delicious Bible Stories*, we presented it to a group with everyone sitting around tables. Each person participated in the preparation of the foods to be tasted. The setup prior to the event took about an hour. Each table has four story bags (see pages 17–19) with the ingredients and the recipes for each of the dishes inside. Each table also has preparation equipment, such as bowls, carafes of water, measuring spoons, and so forth.

Helpful Hint: Allow extra time because the participants talk with one another as they prepare the food. Try not to start the Bible story until everyone is eating, rather than preparing. Remind the participants to turn off their cell phones.

Model #2: One-Time Event in Rows

Time: 1 hour
Script: B (see pages 44–57)
Presenters: 2, 1 hostess and 1 storyteller
Number of participants: As many as the space holds
Plus: Convenient for large groups. All work is done ahead of time, and the participants just listen to the Bible story presentations and "sample" the foods. Easy to clean up after.
Minus: A great deal of pre-event preparation and bag packing

The fourth and fifth times we did *Delicious Bible Stories* were at conferences held in convention centers. Because break-out sessions change so quickly, there is rarely any time to re-arrange a room from one presenter to the next. We had to adapt the event to fit this particular need.

Helpful Hint: Use lidded salad dressing containers (available at most food services outlet stores) for each of the pre-prepared foods. Color code each container and refer in the script to what color container the participants are sampling and what ingredients are included.

Another Helpful Hint: To keep this from being non-participatory other than eating, arrange a few live demonstrations, such as smashing the chickpeas with round river rocks to create the hummus paste.

Model #3: Five Sessions Around Tables

Time: 5 sessions, thirty to forty minutes in length
Script: A (see pages 26–42)
Presenters: 1 hostess and a variety of storytellers
Number of participants: Any number
Plus: The participants aren't rushed. There is plenty of time to get involved in each preparation so that when the time comes for the Bible story, everyone is ready. This works well for Sunday nights, Lenten group studies, or a summer program. It's easier to plan for small groups and one food.

Minus: Pre-event preparation is spread out over five sessions. There is a loss of scope from the time of the patriarchs until the time of the New Testament.

What Is a Story Bag?

In Model #1 and Model #3 of *Delicious Bible Stories*, a story bag is a decorative lunch bag or gift bag for each of these four Bible stories in *Delicious Bible Stories*: Abraham and Sarah, Abigail and David, Queen Esther, and A Wedding at Cana. Use brown paper lunch bags (the most economical) or decorative, handled gift bags (more colorful). Each bag is labeled (see page 63) according to the story for which it will be used. In Model #2, the bag becomes an organizing feature of the presentation. Everything the participants will use or eat is included in the story bag. (See pages 18–19 for contents of the bag.)

What's Inside Model #1 and Model #3 Story Bags?
The most important thing inside each of these story bags is the recipe for the food that each table group will prepare. Make a copy of each story bag recipe for each table (see pages 59–61).

The remaining items in the story bag are the individual containers with the ingredients for the recipe. Label each container and add the pre-measured ingredient.

Why Use a Table Story Bag?
The story bags help organize the amount of "stuff" used in *Delicious Bible Stories*. Using one bag at a time controls the chaos. Some ingredients, such as water, lemon juice, honey, and olive oil, are used in several recipes. Those containers should be on the table, along with measuring cups and spoons. These items will not be listed in the contents of the story bags. During the preparation time, encourage the participants to take turns. It is definitely more fun to share.

Helpful Hint: Use small containers with lids that seal. These are available at food services outlet stores for a reasonable price. They come in large quantities, which you will need; and a sealed container eliminates the possibility of leaking ingredients such as sesame sauce or yogurt.

What's Inside the Story Bag?

Before you can pack a bag, you have to know how many participants to expect. Use the helpful conversion information on page 62 to determine how much of each thing you will need. Then use an assembly line to pack each bag.

Example—The story bag for "Abraham and Sarah" includes:
- the recipe for Classic Hummus (page 59)
- a container of chickpeas with a small plastic bead
- minced garlic (use the pre-prepared, as it's faster)
- tahini (sesame paste)
- a container of pre-measured, ground cumin
- a container of pre-measured paprika
- a container of pre-measured parsley

Containers of water, olive oil, lemon juice, and salt will be available on the table, as well as measuring spoons, a mixing bowl, and a large, round rock for smashing the chickpeas. Also on the table will be a basket of pita bread for tasting and other bowls.

The Story Bag for Model #2

The story bag for the large-group model provides a sampling of the foods for the event. These will be prepared ahead of time and divided among containers for each bag. You will need a bag for each participant. These bags can be packed prior to the event, or the items for the bag can be set out and participants can fill their bags as they come into the room.

Model #2 Story Bag contains:
- two packages of individual hand wipes
- a self-adhesive file folder label

- a plastic fork
- one snack-size resealable baggie with ¼ piece of pita bread
- a container of each of these prepared foods:
  - –hummus (rim of lid marked with red marker)
  - –date cake (rim of lid marked with orange marker)
  - –heart of palm with yogurt sesame sauce (rim of lid marked with green marker)
  - –cheese spread, choose one (rim of lid marked with blue marker)

Who Can Participate?

Delicious Bible Stories can be enjoyed by people of a variety of age levels at the same time. Sharing the preparation tasks around the table can be a fun give-and-take experience for people of all ages.

Elementary children will certainly be interested in the different foods that they will be making and tasting as well as the culture they will learn about. Because these children will be involved in the preparation, they will be more likely to actually taste some of the unfamiliar foods.

Children below the age of five will probably not be able to sit still or remain occupied long enough to make it through the full event. They are also more likely to refuse "odd tasting" foods without a little coaxing. With younger children, choose **Model #3**, the five-session model, instead. Focus on one Bible story at a time.

A Word of Caution: Check with parents about children's food allergies. To prevent spills, if you have young children, select one older person at each table to act as "host" and pour the water over the hands into the bowl, as demonstrated at the beginning.

Youth and adults can enjoy this event right along with the children. The stories are told in a language that is easy to understand for the young ones and with a sense of humor that will appeal to some of the older ones. If you are "going intergenerational," make sure the ages of the participants at each table are mixed. You don't want a table of all children or all adults. The participants will learn from one another as they sample and prepare.

Permit questions as you go along if you feel comfortable with the information. However, in order not to interrupt the flow of the material, put cards on the table so that participants can write down questions to be answered at a later time.

Planning for the Event
The Week Before

Planning ahead is the secret to success for *Delicious Bible Stories*.

Model #1 and Model #2:
If you are using one of these models, you can do only a few things this far in advance.

1. Send out an invitation to advertise the event.

2. Photocopy the Blessing Cards (see page 63, bottom), one of each per table. Use two different colors to prevent confusion.

3. Photocopy the Table Story Bag Labels (see page 63, top), one set for each table.

4. Enlist volunteers to help you fill the story bags. Set a date and time for packing the bags.

5. Purchase grocery and non-grocery items for the event.

6. Locate fabric for costumes for the story characters.

The Day Before

1. Determine the final count of participants.

2. Adjust the recipes on pages 59–61 accordingly (see page 62).

3. Pre-measure the dry ingredients. Store them in small, sealed containers and label them.

4. Grind dates and water into a paste, and put in containers.

5. Make copies of the recipe cards, one for each story bag (see pages 59–61).

6. Set up an assembly line for each story bag. Place the non-perishable items in the appropriate bag. Place all similar bags together in a bin or box.

7. Set up the room.

8. The hostess and the story characters should have a practice read through of the script with the costume changes.

Two Hours Before

1. Measure the yogurt and cream cheese and place in sealed containers. Place them in the appropriate story bags.

2. Double check the story bags to make sure all the necessary items or ingredients are inside.

3. Place the story bags on each table.

4. Cut pita bread circles into quarters. Place one quarter in a sandwich bag. Each participant will need one bag.

5. Place the Blessing Cards (page 63, bottom) on each table.

6. Complete the table settings (see checklist on page 24).

7. Put bulgar wheat in a large bowl. Pour boiling water over it for the Rooster Tabbouleh.

8. Station a greeter at the door to direct participants to their places.

9. Chop tomatoes, yellow pepper, and green onions, and place them in sealed containers. Put in a cooler near (or under) the stage table.

10. Chop chicken into bite-sized pieces (or purchase chicken already cut into bite-sized pieces). Place in a sealed container and put in the cooler near the stage.

Fifteen Minutes Before

1. Set out the costumes in the changing area at the front of the stage.

2. Set out the scripts for the presenter and the guest(s) so that they are easily referred to during the presentation.

3. Place the baskets of pita bread on the tables.

4. Take several deep breaths and say a short prayer, asking God for serenity.

Other Things You Need

In addition to the grocery supplies, you will need:
- four bags for each table
- plastic pitcher and basin and a towel for each table
- hand sanitizer for each table
- containers for olive oil, water, lemon juice, and salt for each table
- sturdy mixing spoons
- a round, smooth rock (for smashing chickpeas) for each table
- cloth or paper napkins for each participant
- a can opener
- a large serving spoon and mixing bowl
- ice chest and ice

If you are doing the event using Model #2, you will not need the first five items. See the packing list for this model on pages 18–19.

Because this is a no-cook event, the number of electrical appliances you will need are limited. You will, however, need a food processor to create the paste from the dried dates.

Front Stage Layout

The Bare Minimum

The front stage area can be as elaborate or as simple as you choose to make it. You will definitely need a six-foot table and at least one chair. Costumes can go on the floor to either the stage right or left. Cover the table with a plastic tablecloth. Slide the cooler with the ingredients for the Rooster Tabbouleh in it under the table. The table also makes a good place to put the scripts so that the storyteller and the hostess can refer to them easily.

If You Have More Space and Time

Create a "talk show" atmosphere with a desk, and easy chair for the storyteller and a table to the side for assembling the final Rooster Tabbouleh. Microphones make it easy for everyone to hear the stories. These are especially nice when you have a large group or a group of children. You will need two of them so that the conversation can go on easily between the hostess and the guests.

Just for Fun

Arrange with someone from the church to record this event with a video camera. It's fun to look back and see all the contortions participants go into as they are smashing chickpeas with a rock or scooping up the hummus with their pita bread.

Individual Table Checklist

✓	ITEMS NEEDED
	pitcher of water
	basin
	one hand towel
	hand sanitizer
	napkins for participants
	basket of pita bread
	container of water
	container of lemon juice
	container of olive oil
	container of honey
	container of salt
	chickpeas in a bowl
	mixing spoons
	mixing bowls
	measuring spoons and cups
	round, smooth rock
	Story Bag #1: Abraham and Sarah
	Story Bag #2: Abigail and David
	Story Bag #3: Queen Esther
	Story Bag #4: The Wedding at Cana

DELICIOUS BIBLE STORIES SCRIPTS

SCRIPT A

for Models #1 & #3

Announcer: Ladies and Gentlemen, welcome to *Delicious Bible Stories*, the show where Bible stories take on a whole new flavor. Let's say hello to our lovely hostess, Rebekah Ray!

Rebekah Ray: Thank you, thank you. Welcome to my kitchen. And thanks to all of you for being here. I am so excited about our show today. We have five wonderful guests who will share with us not only their stories but also their delicious recipes. Trust me, today will be a flavor-filled tour through the Bible. Let's get started, shall we?

Let's begin with our ritual hand washing before eating. This is important because there was no silverware at the Bible-times table.

We have provided the necessary equipment—the pitcher of water, the basin, and the towel. Take turns holding your hands over the basin while another person at the table pours the water over your hands. When everyone has completed the ritual, we will say a special prayer. The prayer is on cards at your table. We will recite the prayer together.

(*Suggested Time: Wait until everyone has washed his or her hands and is seated at the table. Say the Opening Blessing together. This will take about five to ten minutes.*)

Rebekah Ray: Eating with the hands is not the only reason we need to cleanse our hands today. Each of you is going to participate in the preparation of our foods as well as in the eating. It's going to be great fun. So, if you're worried about modern bacteria as we prepare our ancient culinary delights, hand sanitizers are available at each table.

Most of the foods we will be preparing have no hidden ingredients, and there was no MSG in Bible times. For those of you who have food allergies, you are aware of your limitations. We expect you to refrain from eating anything that will cause an allergic reaction, such as the sudden cessation of breathing or extreme gastric distress. Enough said on that. Now, let's gather a little background on our first guest and her tasty dish.

Culinary customs in the Bible began quite simply. People ate the foods that were available. Spices, seasonings, fruits, and vegetables were mostly those things that the people found growing wild or those that could be semi-cultivated as the early nomads traveled from place to place to find food and water for their flocks. The goats and sheep provided the meat, milk, and cheese that was a main portion of their diet. The people supplemented with the wild fruits and vegetables that grew nearby. They did not stay in one place very long, so long-term cultivation of crops was not possible. But a surprising variety was available. Meals were simple and consisted mostly of meats roasted on fire pits, breads baked on heated stones, and fruits and vegetables.

Our first guest today is someone who knows about this early cuisine firsthand. In fact, she prepared and served some of these foods to Abraham, one of the great patriarchs of Old Testament times. Let's put our clean hands together for Sarah's Servant!

(Sarah's Servant ENTERS.)

Sarah's Servant: Today, we *(gestures to all the people in the audience)* are going to prepare and enjoy a tasty recipe that I have fixed many times as we traveled in the wilderness. In fact, it was a favorite of Abraham and Sarah. Abraham even served it to three special guests who came to our tents one day. But I'm getting ahead of myself.

Rebekah Ray: Right. Audience, find the bag on your table marked "Abraham and Sarah." Take out the recipe card and all the ingredients inside. Follow the recipe. Work together to make Classic Hummus. All of you will create four recipes today, so make sure everyone has a chance to participate in the preparation.

Sarah's Servant: Before you go any farther, the very first thing you need to do is drain the chickpeas into one of the bowls. Check to make sure there are no rocks or pebbles mixed in with the chickpeas.

Once that is done, smash up those little peas with your rock. Yes, I did say rock. That is the method the people in my day and time used to crush, smash, and grind all of our foods. Once the mixture looks like mashed potatoes, add the rest of the ingredients. Mmm. Doesn't the whole room smell good? When all of the mixing is completed, pass around the pita bread. Each person at the table should take one piece. Break your bread into several pieces. The bread will become your eating utensil for today. Don't eat all your bread at once; otherwise, you won't have any for later dishes.

Rebekah Ray: I'm getting hungry already. Nothing I like better than chickpeas and garlic.

*(**Suggested Time:** Give the tables about five to ten minutes to prepare the hummus dish. Remind them to find the pebbles. Do not begin the story until all the preparation is completed.)*

Sarah's Servant: Remember, you must use only your right hand for eating, even if you are left handed. The left hand was never used for eating; it was used only for other bodily functions.

Break off a small piece of your pita bread and scoop up some hummus. Remember, no double dipping! If you want a second dip, you must break off another piece of the bread. Close your eyes as those wonderful flavors fill your mouth. Yum!

Rebekah Ray: Now, please tell us your story as they eat.

Sarah's Servant: My story begins late one afternoon. Three travelers came to our encampment. It was as if they had come from nowhere! One minute there was no one on the road. Then, suddenly, there they were. Out in the wilderness, we don't see many travelers. So whenever someone comes your way, you treat him with special care. And we had three!

Abraham rushed to meet them. He greeted them in the traditional way. He bowed slightly, raised his right hand to touch his forehead, his lips, and his heart. Nothing else would be done until the greeting was completed.

Let's give that a try. Everyone, stand up. Now bow, touch your right hand to your forehead, your lips, and your heart. Great. Sit back down. (Laughs.) At Abraham's age, it was a wonder he could bow at all. But he was the perfect host. He offered the visitors a place to sit in the shade of a tree. Then he gave them water to drink.

Abraham ordered the servants to prepare some food for them. Abraham wanted them to stay and share any news they had. Out here in the wilderness, you sort of lose touch.

While the herdsmen prepared a calf for roasting, the other servant girls and I busily prepared a bowl of hummus, very much like the one you just sampled. This would tide them over until the real meal was ready.

Eating went on for hours. The more they ate, the more they talked. The more they talked, the more they ate. At one point during the meal, one of the men turned to Abraham and said something very strange. That's when it happened.

Rebekah Ray: What happened?

Sarah's Servant: The silent laugh that was heard through the Bible!

Rebekah Ray: Silent laugh?

Sarah's Servant: Yes. While the men were chatting, we women were listening at the tent divide (looking slightly embarrassed). We couldn't eat with them, but we **could** listen to the conversation. After all, we didn't want to miss a thing.

Classic Hummus

See the recipe on page 59.

29

The man told Abraham that Sarah was going to have a baby. First of all, I wondered if he had seen Sarah and knew how old she was. Who has a baby when she is ninety-something years old? Then I wondered how Sarah was taking the news. I couldn't hear her or see her face, but I could see her shoulders shaking with laughter.

The man called her to come out from the tent. How embarrassing! He asked her why she had laughed. Sarah denied having laughed at all. But somehow the man knew. And then he did it.

Rebekah Ray: Did what?

Sarah's Servant: Made the promise!

Rebekah Ray: The promise? *(getting very interested)* What kind of promise?

Sarah's Servant: The man told Sarah that next year, at this very time, he would come by Abraham's tents once again and, when he did, Sarah would have a child.

Rebekah Ray: And…and…and… *(She motions for girl to hurry up and continue the story.)*

Sarah's Servant: It happened, just as he had said. I mean, God had promised Abraham and Sarah many years before that they were going to have children. But so many years had gone by. I think they had just given up. But now, there was hope.

One year later, Sarah and Abraham had a beautiful baby boy. They named him Isaac, which, of course you know, means "he laughs." This time Sarah wasn't laughing silently; she was laughing out loud with sheer joy.

Rebekah Ray: What a wonderful and unexpected story. Did you ever discover who those men were?

Sarah's Servant: We never did know for sure, but everyone believes that one of the three men was the Lord himself.

Rebekah Ray: Wow! God in person. What an exciting story. Thank you for sharing it with us today. And let me confess, that appetizer was quite delicious. How about that, folks *(turns to audience)*, another delicious Bible story.

(Sarah's Servant EXITS.)

Rebekah Ray: Our next guest is a behind-the-scenes woman you hear very little about. She is not only a great hostess and cook, but she is also known in the inner circles of the royal court as a peacemaker. Her name is Abigail. She has an interesting tale to tell us today. It seems Abigail had an encounter with **David** *(emphasize word)*. Yes, we're talking about **that** David, the obscure shepherd boy whose meteoric rise to fame is the stuff legends are made from. She's here to share a little inside info about the most famous and most beloved king of all of Israel. Let's hear it for Abigail, widow of Nabal, the sheep farmer, and the future wife of King David himself.

STORY 2

(Abigail ENTERS.)

Rebekah Ray: Welcome to our show, Abigail. We are delighted you were able to make it today.

Abigail: I'm so glad to be here. Actually, after you hear my story, you'll understand why I'm just glad to be anywhere. At one point, I thought that my life was coming to an abrupt end.

Rebekah Ray: That is intriguing. It sounds life changing.

Abigail: It was actually life saving. And I owe my life to my fig cakes. I call them the fig cakes that stopped a war.

Rebekah Ray: That does sound interesting. I can hardly wait to hear your story and taste your fig cakes. First things first. Let's start with the fig cakes. We have some wonderful folks here in the studio audience who will help us re-create them. Everyone, find the bag marked "Abigail and David." Carefully remove all the ingredients and the recipe.

Please note that you have dates instead of figs. Figs are more expensive than dates, so we made a substitution. Both fruits were available, however, in Old Testament times.

Abigail: One of the containers on your table contains a paste of ground dates. Use a mixing spoon to scrape this out into your larger bowl.

Now follow your recipe. When the mixture begins to stick together, scoop out a small amount and roll it into a ball. Pour a little honey onto your plate. Roll the ball in the honey and then in some of the chopped almonds.

Take your time. Chew it slowly. You will want to savor all those delicious flavors—cinnamon, cardamom, dates, walnuts, and almonds. A real treat!

Rachel Ray: Heavenly. Now as the group is enjoying your cakes, let's hear the real story behind them and what made them the cakes that prevented a war.

Abigail's Date Cakes

See the recipe on page 60.

Abigail: My husband, Nabal, owned thousands of sheep. Once a year, we would shear them and take their wool to be used for clothing and blankets. It was a time for celebrating. Everyone was included.

David, who wasn't king yet, was traveling with his men through the area. It had been some time since they had really eaten a meal, so they sent word to Nabal and asked if they could be included in the festivities. That seemed fair, since they had been protecting our herders from bandits and rustlers.

But Nabal—*(to audience)* did I tell you that his name means "fool"?—sent word back to David, saying in effect, "No way. You are not welcome."

Hospitality was something that was expected in Bible times. You'd think Nabal would have known that. David had been rather polite in his request. Unfortunately, Nabal had been rather rude in his response. Nabal didn't even consider the fact that David was traveling with a band of soldiers.

When David got Nabal's response, he became *so* angry. He called his men together and prepared for war. This time they would *take* what they wanted and *kill* everyone as well.

Fortunately, I have a wise servant who came to me and told me what had happened. I knew I had to do something—fast.

So, I ordered the servants to put together a small caravan of food. It was simple fare, really—meat, bread, raisins, wine, and measures of grain. I also had them include some of my famous fig cakes. We set out to find David and his men. I hoped I was not too late.

We met David and his men on their way to attack the farm. I jumped from the donkey and threw myself at his feet. I wasn't opposed to a little groveling, if it would save lives.

I apologized for my ill-mannered husband. I begged David to accept my gifts of food for himself and for his men—a peace offering, if you will. David was ever so grateful. My act of generosity and hospitality had prevented David from taking revenge upon Nabal and all of the people of our household. But I prefer to believe it was my fig cakes that turned the tide.

Rachel Ray: Fig cakes that prevented a war. I don't believe I've ever heard that one before. But on your bio, it says you became one of David's wives. How did that happen?

Abigail: Well *(roll eyes and look coy)*, once Nabal had come to his senses, I told him what had happened. The stress of the whole thing was too much for him. His heart stopped beating and he died. When David heard about my husband's death, he decided a woman with such a cool head…

Rebekah Ray: And delicious fig cakes…

Abigail: And delicious fig cakes deserved a new life. So he sent for me and made me his wife.

Rebekah Ray: How romantic! Thus ends another happily-ever-after delicious Bible story.

(Abigail EXITS.)

Rebekah Ray: I don't think anyone can top that story. But our next guest is surely going to try. Let's jump ahead a few centuries now.

When David finally became the king, he united the countries of Israel and Judah into one powerful nation. The people of the land had a time of relative prosperity. Under David's son Solomon, Israel became a center of culture. But with all the prosperity, the people moved God to the sidelines. The prophets warned the people that they were headed in the wrong direction. But they didn't listen. Israel has always been stubborn.

Because God was no longer at the center of their life, the country became weak and divided. All it took was one small Babylonian army swooping in from the east, and it all came to an end. To add insult to injury, the Babylonian army not only sacked the cities and burned the Temple, but the army also took the brightest of the people back with them to Babylon. That's where our next guest is from. Let's welcome to our show today true royalty—Queen Esther.

STORY
3

(Queen Esther ENTERS.)

Rebekah Ray: *(She tries to curtsy, but does so awkwardly and falls over.)* Welcome, Queen Esther. We're honored you're here. We've never had a queen on the show before. We look forward to hearing your story and sampling that unbelievably tasty Persian cuisine. If I'm not mistaken, your delicious Bible story is told every year at the Jewish festival of Purim, isn't it?

Queen Esther: Yes, it is, Rebekah Ray. It is a timeless story. It is a story about love. A story about palace intrigue. A story about communication between a husband and a wife. My story proves that some things just don't change.

Rebekah Ray: We want to hear every delightful and delicious word of it, so let's get started. What scrumptious treat did you bring?

Queen Esther: Being a young Jewish girl, I come from a tradition of simple, healthful meals where vegetables play an important role. This was not always the case in Babylon. In fact, sometimes things got out of hand, like the banquet that went on for six months. The recipe I brought for you today is not only tasty, but is good for you as well.

Rebekah Ray: Everyone, let's find the bag labeled "Queen Esther." Remove all the items from inside.

Queen Esther: Just follow the recipe in your bag to make the sauce. When you've finished, take a small piece of the heart of palm and put it on your plate. Spoon some sauce over it. Yum!

Rebekah Ray: Sauces are my life. This one is quite unusual. As we sample, tell us your story.

Queen Esther: Before I was queen, I was just an ordinary, exceedingly beautiful, modest Jewish girl living in Babylon. One day the king was having a great banquet. He was feeling a bit show-offish and ordered Queen Vashti to drop what she was doing and come to the banquet. He wanted her to entertain the men who were there.

This didn't sit well with Vashti, who was hosting a banquet for the women elsewhere in the palace. So she sent word that she was busy.

Yogurt Sesame
Sauce Over
Hearts of Palm

See the recipe on page 60.

35

Not many queens refuse their husband's direct orders—not and live, anyway. The king deposed her and set about looking for a new queen.

That's where I come in. My cousin Mordecai suggested that I try out for the position. I was sure that there were many more beautiful women in the kingdom who wanted to be queen. But I was wrong. When the king laid eyes on me, it was love at first sight. So, I was selected as the next queen.

Now, the king was not aware of one small, teeny-weeny problem I had. I was Jewish. Jewish people were outcasts in the kingdom at this time. I wasn't quite sure what to do. Mordecai told me not to mention it, so I didn't.

Everything was going along fine. Then one day Mordecai overheard a plot by one of the king's advisors, a man named Haman. Haman planned to have our people killed. Mordecai pleaded with me to intercede with the king. I was terrified. But if I didn't, who would save the people?

But what Mordecai didn't understand was that you simply didn't drop in on the king without an invitation. But dead is dead. What did I have to lose?

So I steeled myself and went to the throne room. To my surprise—tee-hee, not really—the king was delighted to see me. I invited him and his chief advisor, who happened to be the perpetrator of the plot, to a banquet.

That night, once he and Haman had been royally fed—my hearts of palm with yogurt sesame sauce was one of the dishes—I told my husband what his advisor had planned for me and my people. My husband was furious.

Needless to say, my people were saved and Haman lost his job—and his life. I'm sure it had to do with my exceptionally good food and inspirational company.

Rebekah Ray: I totally agree, Queenie. You are one brave woman. And we are delighted that you are alive and that you were willing to share your delicious Bible story with us.

(Queen Esther EXITS.)

Rebekah Ray: Everybody loves a wedding, and this was true even in Bible times. A wedding was a major village event. The festivities included music, dancing, poetry-reading, food, and, of course, plenty of wine.

The wedding took place at the bridegroom's house. The groom would take his entourage to the bride's house, where the bride would be waiting with her bridesmaids. Then the bridegroom would escort the bridal party back to his house for the celebration. All the people dressed in the finest clothes they had. In fact, it was an insult to wear anything less than your best.

When the procession arrived at the groom's house, there was the ritual washing of hands. Families kept large jars of water just for this purpose. Then the festivities would begin and would last sometimes for a whole week.

Our next guest is going to give us a firsthand account of one of these wedding feasts in the quaint little town of Cana. Let's welcome the bridesmaid.

STORY
4

(Bridesmaid ENTERS.)

Bridesmaid: Thank you, thank you. As you said, Rebekah Ray, everyone loves a wedding. And I brought along some of the ingredients for you to make a delicious wedding treat. I'm hoping some day to be able to use these recipes at my own wedding.

Rebekah Ray: What are we waiting for? Let's get started.

Bridesmaid: Today, we're going to make three flavored cheese spreads: cinnamon, black cumin seed, and horseradish. Not every table will be making all three, so you're going to need to share your cheese spread with another table. Just remove the ingredients from the bag marked "A Wedding at Cana" and combine them together in the bowl. Mix well so that the flavors spread throughout the cheese.

When you've created your cheese spread, scoop some out on a small plate and share that plate with another table. Please be careful and don't mix the cheese spreads together. Use your pita bread to eat it.

(*Suggested Time: Allow about five to ten minutes for the cheese spreads to be completed, shared, and sampled.*)

Cheese Spreads
See the recipe on page 61.

Rebekah Ray: These are positively delicious! While we're sampling, go ahead and give us the details about this wedding at Cana. Was it anyone famous? Anyone we'd recognize?

Bridesmaid: I don't think so; but, let me tell you, I will never forget it. I mean, I witnessed a true miracle!

Rebekah Ray: A miracle! Are you sure?

Bridesmaid: Yes, a miracle. It couldn't be anything else. There is no other way to explain it.

Rebekah Ray: Don't keep us in suspense.

Bridesmaid: The wedding festivities had been going on for days. It was the best—the best food, the best music, the best wine. But then with a couple of days still left, the wine steward noticed that the bridegroom was running out of wine. This would be a disaster! Running out of wine would be a real social faux pas.

One of the guests was Mary of Nazareth. She had come with her son Jesus and his group of friends. Mary turned to her son and told him to "fix the problem." I had overheard part of this and wondered just what he was going to be able to do to "fix it." Did he bring a couple of extra jugs of wine with him?

At first Jesus was reluctant. More than that, he was rather put out with his mother. I overheard him tell her that it wasn't his time yet. Time for what, I don't know. But his mother just gave him that look—you know the look mother's are so good at. So Jesus told the servants to fill the ceremonial jars with water. When that was done, he had a servant draw a cup of water from a jar and give it to the wine steward to taste. Yuck! I certainly hoped he wasn't going to suggest drinking it instead of wine. The hand-washing water? I don't think so!

The wine steward lifted the cup to his nose and sniffed and sniffed again. Then he tasted the water. His eyes got big and round. He turned to Jesus. I could tell even then that what he was drinking was not water at all, but the VERY best wine—even better than the wine they had served at the beginning of the feast.

Rebekah Ray: Whoa! Wait just a minute. Water into wine? How did that happen?

Bridesmaid: All I know is that one minute it was water and the next minute it was wine. Jesus did it. Jesus turned the water into wine. If that's not a miracle, I don't know what is.

Rebekah Ray: Wow! What a delicious story. Thanks for sharing it with us today.

(Bridesmaid EXITS.)

Rebekah Ray: Now for our final guest and the main course.

My producers have told me that we are going to prepare a very special poultry-based salad. I think they got the name wrong, but we'll let our next guest set us straight.

Let's give a warm welcome to the Servant Girl from Caiaphas' courtyard.

(Servant Girl ENTERS.)

Servant Girl: Thank you, Rebekah Ray. I'm delighted to be here and share my recipe for Rooster Tabbouleh Salad With Mint.

Rebekah Ray: Rooster Salad? Then my producers got it right. But don't people usually say "chicken salad" instead?

Servant Girl: They might, unless they had been with me in the courtyard at Caiaphas' house. Shall we get started?

(Servant Girl and Rebekah make the Rooster Tabbouleh Salad together.)

Servant Girl: First, we add bulgur wheat that's been soaking in hot water. The soaking makes it tender. Add those chopped tomatoes. Aren't they pretty? So red and ripe and tasty.

Rebekah Ray: Yum, tasty.

Servant Girl: Now put in some of that colorful pepper, some green onions, and the seasonings—mint, parsley, salt, and pepper. Stir it well. Add the olive oil, and drizzle in a little lemon juice.

Now it's time for the rooster. Rebekah Ray, you do the honors.

Rebekah Ray: Wherever did you find fresh rooster?

Servant Girl: Oh, I found it early one morning in the courtyard. In fact, that's how my story begins.

Rebekah Ray: By all means, continue as we serve your Rooster Tabbouleh. We eat it with the romaine leaves, right?

Servant Girl: Yes, that's right.

(**Suggested Time:** *Allow five to ten minutes to dish out the salad.*)

Rebekah Ray: Now that everyone has been served, let's hear this story.

Servant Girl: I serve the high priest of the Temple in Jerusalem. His name is Caiaphas. My story begins on the evening of the Passover meal. That night, long after everyone else had gone to bed, there was a great commotion in the courtyard. The Temple guards had arrested a man named Jesus and brought him here for trial.

Rooster Tabbouleh
Salad With Mint

See the recipe on page 61.

I had heard about this man. Caiaphas and his group of priests thought he was a troublemaker. They thought he was sure to bring the Romans down on them. But he didn't look like that kind of man. And I had heard that he was able to do wonderful things, such as changing water into wine.

Rebekah Ray: Yes, I've heard that rumor too.

Servant Girl: So, while Caiaphas gathered the members of the council together, people began to crowd into the courtyard to see what was going on. As I was standing near the fire, I thought I recognized one of the men. I had seen him with this man Jesus before, maybe in the marketplace. I called him out.

But he denied it, saying, "No! I don't know this Jesus."

Then several others joined the conversation. They thought they recognized him as well. But each time, the man denied even knowing Jesus and moved farther away into the shadows.

Suddenly, everything got quiet. There it was. The rooster crowed. It was almost morning. The man in question ran from the courtyard. He looked as if he had lost his best friend.

Rebekah Ray: That's a very moving story. Did you ever find out what happened to the man, Jesus?

Servant Girl: Yes, but that's another story.

Rebekah Ray: Unfortunately, we are out of time for today. Let's close our meal with the final hand washing. When everyone is finished, we'll say our Closing Blessing together.

(Guests wash hands and recite the Closing Blessing.)

Rebekah Ray: Tune in tomorrow as we continue our delicious Bible stories. Our guest will be Mary Magdalene, a dear close friend of the man Jesus. She will be sharing her very special bread recipe, Resurrection Rolls.

This is Rebekah Ray wishing you your own delicious encounters with the Bible stories.

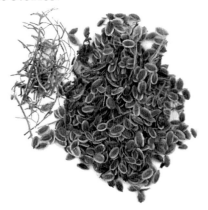

42

Model #2: Large Group

Making the Presentation Interactive

The preparation and presentation of *Delicious Bible Stories* for this model is slightly different than it would be if the participants were gathered around tables. Most of the dialogue remains the same, except for the introduction to the stories. We have added participatory movement so that the audience can be an integral part of the storytelling.

Food Bags: Each bag for this model will need these items

- ¼ pita bread in a plastic bag
- 2 hand wipes
- plastic fork
- food containers
- Opening Blessing and Closing Blessing (see page 63)
- file labels
- three or four pennies

Preparation:
- Prepare the food recipes in advance (see pages 59–61), except for the Rooster Tabbouleh. Choose only one of the cheese spread recipes.

- Divide the food into lidded containers, one container for each participant.

- Color code the lids using permanent felt-tip markers.

Serving the Food: Either
- Pack the food bags ahead of time. Place the bags in large boxes or bins. Participants will take a bag as they come into the room.

- Put each item in a separate bin. Allow participants to pick up one of each item (except for the hand wipes, of which they need two).

SCRIPT B

for Model #2

Announcer: Ladies and Gentlemen, welcome to *Delicious Bible Stories*, the show where Bible stories take on a whole new flavor. Let's say hello to our lovely hostess, Rebekah Ray.

Rebekah Ray: Thank you, thank you. Welcome to my kitchen. And thanks to all of you for being here. I am so excited about our show today. We have five wonderful guests who will share with us not only their stories but also their delicious recipes. Trust me, today will be a flavor-filled tour through the Bible. Let's get started, shall we?

Of course, as we do at the beginning of every program, we need to begin with our ritual hand washing before eating. We do this mostly because there was no silverware allowed at the Bible-times table. My helper and I will demonstrate how this is done. (*Alternately hold hands over the basin and pour the water over the hands. Then dry with a towel.*)

You will find hand wipes in your bags so that you can clean your hands. Now that we have completed that, we will begin with a special prayer that accompanies each hand washing.

Blessed art thou, Jehovah, our God, King of the world, who causes to come forth bread from the earth. Amen.

Most of the foods we will be preparing have no hidden ingredients, and there was no MSG in Bible times. For those of you who have food allergies, you are aware of your limitations. We expect you to refrain from eating anything that will cause an allergic reaction, such as the sudden cessation of breathing or extreme gastric distress. Enough said on that. Now, let's gather a little background on our first guest and her tasty dish.

Culinary customs in Bible times began quite simply. People ate the foods that were available. Spices, seasonings, fruits, and vegetables were mostly those things that the people found growing wild or were semi-cultivated as the early nomads traveled from place to place to find food and water for their flocks. The goats and sheep provided the meat, milk, and cheese that was a main portion of their diet. The people supplemented with the wild fruits and vegetables that grew nearby. They did not stay in one place very long, so long-term cultivation of crops was not possible. But a surprising variety was available. Meals were simple and consisted mostly of meats roasted on fire pits, breads baked on heated stones, and fruits and vegetables.

Our first guest today is someone who knows about this early cuisine firsthand. In fact, she prepared and served some of these foods to Abraham, one of the great patriarchs of Old Testament times. Let's put our clean hands together for Sarah's Servant Girl!

STORY

1

(Sarah's Servant ENTERS.)

Sarah's Servant: Today, we *(gestures to all the people in the audience)* are going to prepare and enjoy a tasty recipe that I have fixed many times as we traveled in the wilderness. In fact, it was a favorite of Abraham and Sarah. Abraham even served it to three special guests who came to our tents one day. But I'm getting ahead of myself.

First of all, I would like to demonstrate how difficult food preparation was in Bible times. I need some volunteers. There are bowls and rocks placed throughout the room. *(Invite participants to go to a bowl.)* I want to see how smooth you can make your chickpeas. First, make sure there are no rocks or pebbles mixed in with the chickpeas. *(Beads have been placed in the chickpeas to represent pebbles.)* Then smash the chickpeas with a rock. Not a lump should show. Makes you appreciate the conveniences of modern times, doesn't it? For example, the food processor.

Rebekah Ray: Right. Audience, find the container in your bag with the **red rim**. This is what we like to call Classic Hummus. It has already been prepared for you. In a plastic baggie, you will find pita bread in your bag. Break off a piece of bread and scoop up some of the hummus. You will need to save the rest of the bread for later tasty treats. And, of course, use only your right hand for eating. The left hand was never used for eating; it was used only for other bodily functions.

(As everyone is sampling, continue.)

Rebekah Ray: Now, you can continue to eat as we hear the story that goes along with our hummus.

Servant Girl: My story begins late one afternoon. Three travelers came to our encampment. It was as if they had come from nowhere! One minute there was no one on the road. Then, suddenly, there they were. Out in the wilderness, we don't see many travelers. So whenever one comes your way, you treat him with special care. And we had three!

Abraham rushed to meet them. He greeted them in the traditional way. He bowed slightly *(demonstrate)*, raised his right hand to touch his forehead *(demonstrate)*, his lips *(demonstrate)*, and his heart *(demonstrate)*. Nothing else would be done until the greeting was completed.

Let's give that a try. Everyone, stand up. Now bow, touch your right hand to your forehead, your lips, and your heart. Great. Sit back down. As I continue the story, listen for the name **Abraham**. When you hear me say my master's name, stand up and do the greeting. Then sit back down.

Abraham offered them places to sit in the shade and water to drink. He ordered us to prepare some food for them. **Abraham** wanted them to stay and share any news. Out here in the wilderness, you sort of lose touch.

While the herdsmen prepared a calf for roasting, the other servant girls and I busily prepared the hummus dish you just sampled. This would tide them over until the real meal was ready. Eating went on for hours. The more they ate the more they talked. The more they talked, the more they ate. At one point, one of the men turned to **Abraham** and said something very strange. That's when it happened.

Rebekah Ray: What happened?

Sarah's Servant: The silent laugh that was heard throughout the Bible!

Rebekah Ray: Silent laugh?

Sarah's Servant: Yes. While **Abraham** and the men were chatting, we women were listening at the tent divide. We didn't want to miss a thing. The man told **Abraham** that Sarah was going to have a baby. First of all, I wondered if he had seen Sarah and knew how old she was. Who has a baby when she is ninety-something years old? Then I wondered how Sarah was taking the news. I couldn't see her face, but I could see her shoulders shaking with laughter.

I had not heard her and don't see how anyone else could have, but the man obviously had. He called her to come out from the tent. How embarrassing! He asked her why she had laughed. Sarah denied it. But somehow the man knew. That's when he made the promise.

Rebekah Ray: The promise? *(getting very interested)* What kind of promise?

Sarah's Servant: The man told Sarah that next year, at this very time, he would come by **Abraham's** tents once again and, when he did, Sarah would have a child.

Rebekah Ray: And...and...and... *(She motions for girl to continue.)*

Sarah's Servant: It happened, just as he had said. I mean, God had promised **Abraham** and Sarah many years before that they were going to have children. But so many years had gone by. I think they had just given up. But now, Sarah and **Abraham** had hope again. One year later, Sarah and

Abraham had a beautiful baby boy. They named him Isaac, which, of course you know, means "he laughs." This time Sarah wasn't laughing silently; she was laughing out loud with sheer joy.

Rebekah Ray: What a wonderful and unexpected story. Did you ever discover who those men were?

Sarah's Servant: Everyone believes that one of the three whom Abraham greeted was the Lord.

Rebekah Ray: Wow! God in person. What an exciting story. Thank you for sharing it with us today. And let me confess, that appetizer was quite delicious. How about that, folks *(turns to audience)*, another delicious Bible story.

(Sarah's Servant EXITS.)

Rebekah Ray: Our next guest is a behind-the-scenes woman you hear very little about. She is not only a great hostess and cook, but she is also known in the inner circles of the royal court as a peacemaker. Her name is Abigail. She has an interesting tale to tell us today. It seems Abigail had an encounter with **David** *(emphasize word)*. Yes, we're talking about **that** David, the obscure shepherd boy whose meteoric rise to fame is the stuff legends are made from. She's here to share a little inside info about the most famous and most beloved king of all of Israel. Let's hear it for Abigail, widow of Nabal, the sheep farmer, and the future wife of King David himself.

STORY 2

(Abigail ENTERS.)

Rebekah Ray: Welcome to our show, Abigail. We are delighted you were able to make it today.

Abigail: I'm so glad to be here. Actually, after you hear my story, you'll understand why I'm just glad to be anywhere. At one point, I thought my life was coming to an abrupt end.

Rebekah Ray: That is intriguing. It sounds life changing.

Abigail: It was actually life saving. And I owe my life to my fig cakes. I call them the fig cakes that stopped a war.

Rebekah Ray: Interesting. I can hardly wait to hear your story and taste your fig cakes. First things first. Locate the container with the **orange rim**. Inside, you will find a sample of the delicious cakes.

Please note that you have dates instead of figs. Figs are considerably more expensive than dates, so a substitution was in order. Both fruits were equally available, however, in Old Testament times.

Abigail: Before I start my story, I want to remind you who David was. God chose him, even though he was the youngest of Jesse's sons, to be king after Saul—not because of his good looks (although he was quite handsome), but because of his heart. David is the shepherd boy who used his sling to protect his sheep from wild animals. And, of course, he's the boy who used that same sling to kill Goliath. So as I tell the story, let's honor David. When you hear me say the name **David**, raise your arm over your head and move it in a circle as if you are twirling a sling. Give it a try. *(Have the participants do the motion.)*

My husband, Nabal, owned thousands of sheep. Once a year, we sheared them. It was a time of celebration for everyone.

David, who wasn't king yet, was traveling with his men through the area. It had been some time since they had really eaten a meal, so **David** sent word to Nabal and asked if they could be included in the festivities. That seemed fair, since they had been protecting our herders from bandits.

But Nabal—*(to audience)* did I tell you that his name means "fool"?—sent word back to **David**, saying, "No way."

Hospitality was expected in Bible times. You'd think Nabal would have known that. **David** had been rather polite in his request, but Nabal had been rather rude in his response.

49

David called his men together and prepared for war. This time they would *take* what they wanted and *kill* everyone as well.

Fortunately, I have a quick-thinking servant who told me what had happened. I knew I had to do something—fast.

So, I ordered the servants to put together a small caravan of food—meat, bread, raisins, wine, and measures of grain. I also had them include some of my famous fig cakes. We set out to find **David** and his men. I hoped I was not too late.

We met **David** and his men on their way to attack the farm. I jumped from the donkey and threw myself at his feet. I wasn't opposed to a little groveling, if it would save lives.

I apologized for my ill-mannered husband. I begged **David** to accept my gifts of food—a peace offering, if you will. **David** was grateful. My act of generosity and hospitality had prevented him from taking revenge upon Nabal and our household. But I prefer to believe it was my fig cakes that turned the tide.

Rachel Ray: Fig cakes that prevented a war. I don't believe I've ever heard that one before. But on your bio, it says you became one of **David's** wives. How did that happen?

Abigail: Well *(roll eyes and look coy)*, once Nabal had come to his senses, I told him what had happened. The stress of the whole thing was too much for him. His heart stopped beating and he died. When **David** heard about my husband's death, he decided a woman with such a cool head…

Rebekah Ray: And delicious fig cakes…

Abigail: And delicious fig cakes deserved a new life. So he sent for me and made me his wife.

Rebekah Ray: How romantic! Thus ends another happily-ever-after delicious Bible story.

(Abigail EXITS.)

Rebekah Ray: I don't think anyone can top that story. But our next guest is surely going to try. Let's jump ahead a few centuries now.

When David finally became the king, he united the countries of Israel and Judah into one nation. The people of the land had a time of prosperity. Under David's son Solomon, Israel became a cultural center. But with the prosperity, the people moved God to the sidelines. The prophets warned the people, but they didn't listen.

Because God was no longer at the center of their life, the country became weak and divided. All it took was one small Babylonian army swooping in from the east, and it all came to an end. To add insult to injury, the Babylonian army not only sacked the cities and burned the Temple, but they also took the brightest of the people back with them to Babylon. That's where our next guest is from. Let's welcome to our show true royalty—Queen Esther.

(Queen Esther ENTERS.)

Rebekah Ray: *(She tries to curtsy, but does so awkwardly and falls over.)* Welcome, Queen Esther. We're honored you're here. We've never had a queen on the show before. We look forward to hearing your story and sampling that unbelievably tasty Persian cuisine. If I'm not mistaken, your delicious Bible story is told every year at the Jewish festival of Purim, isn't it?

Queen Esther: Yes, it is, Rebekah Ray. It is a timeless story. It is a story about love. A story about palace intrigue. A story about communication between a husband and a wife. My story proves that some things just don't change.

Rebekah Ray: Everyone, find the container with the **green rim**. You can use your fork to sample this delicious treat. I know we said that we would use no silverware, but we just don't want to eat this with our fingers. As we sample, tell us your story.

Queen Esther: I'd love to, but let's use a custom from the festival of Purim. Take the label from your bag. Write the name Haman on the label. Now, stick the label on the bottom of your shoe. Every time I say the name **Haman**—he's the bad guy—stomp your foot. In my time the streets were littered with refuse and mud; so when you walked in the street, the bottom of your shoes became filthy. To put someone's name there was a true insult.

Before I was queen, I was just an ordinary, exceedingly beautiful, modest Jewish girl living in Babylon. One day the king was having a great banquet. He was feeling a bit show-offish and ordered Queen Vashti to drop what she was doing and come to the banquet to entertain the men.

But Vashti, who was hosting a banquet for the women elsewhere in the palace, sent word that she was too busy. Not many queens refuse the king's direct orders—not and live, anyway. And so the king set about looking for a new queen.

That's where I come in. My cousin Mordecai suggested that I try out for the position. I was sure that there were many more beautiful women in Babylon who wanted to be queen. But I was wrong. When the king laid eyes on me, it was love at first sight. So, I was selected as the next queen.

Everything was going along fine. Then one day Mordecai overheard a plot by one of the king's advisors, a man named **Haman**. **Haman** planned to have our people killed. Mordecai pleaded with me to intercede with the king. I was terrified. But if I didn't, who would save the people from **Haman's** plot?

Now, you could be killed for dropping in on the king without an invitation. But dead is dead. What did I have to lose? So I steeled myself and went to the throne room. Thankfully, the king was delighted to see me. I invited him and **Haman,** the perpetrator of the plot, to a banquet.

Once he and **Haman** had been royally fed—my hearts of palm with yogurt sesame sauce was one of the dishes—I told my husband what **Haman** had planned for me and my people. My husband was furious. Needless to say, my people were saved and **Haman** lost his job—and his life. I'm sure it had to do with my exceptionally good food and inspirational company.

Rebekah Ray: I totally agree, Queenie. You are one brave woman. And we are delighted that you are alive and that you were willing to share your delicious Bible story with us.

(Queen Esther EXITS.)

Rebekah Ray: Everybody loves a wedding, and this was true even in Bible times. A wedding was a major village event that included music, dancing, food, and, of course, plenty of wine.

The wedding took place at the bridegroom's house. The groom would take his entourage to the bride's house, where the bride would be waiting with her bridesmaids. Then the bridegroom would escort the bridal party back to his house for the celebration.

Everyone was dressed in their finest. In fact, it was an insult to wear anything less than your best. The bride usually wore ten silver coins hung across her forehead. These were given to her by her mother or her groom. They were like an engagement ring. To lose even one of these coins was devastating. Remember the story of the lost coin?

Take out the coins from your bag. Hold them in your hand. Every time you hear the word **wedding**, shake your coins.

When the **wedding** procession arrived at the groom's house, there was the ritual washing of hands. Families kept large jars of water just for this purpose alone. Then the week-long **wedding** festivities would begin. Our next guest took part in one of these **wedding** feasts. Let's welcome the bridesmaid.

(Bridesmaid ENTERS.)

Bridesmaid: Thank you, thank you. As you said, Rebekah Ray, everyone loves a **wedding**. And I brought along one of the common dishes served at a **wedding** in Bible times. I'm hoping some day to be able to use this recipe at my own **wedding**.

Rebekah Ray: What are we waiting for? Let's get started. Locate the container in your bag with the **blue rim**. This is a flavored cheese spread. Use your pita bread to sample it.

(Pause while the cheese is being sampled.)

Rebekah Ray: Delicious! While we're sampling, go ahead and give us the details about this **wedding**. I believe it was at Cana?

Bridesmaid: Yes, Cana. Well, let me tell you, I will never forget it. I mean, I witnessed a true miracle!

Rebekah Ray: A miracle! Are you sure?

Bridesmaid: Yes, a miracle. It couldn't be anything else.

Rebekah Ray: Don't keep us in suspense.

Bridesmaid: The **wedding** festivities had been going on for days. It was the best—the best food, the best music, the best wine. But then with a couple of days still left, the wine steward noticed that they were running out of wine. What a disaster! Running out of wine at a **wedding**! Talk about a social faux pas.

One of the **wedding** guests was Mary of Nazareth. She had come with her son Jesus and his group of friends. Mary turned to her son and told him to "fix the problem." I had overheard part of this and wondered how he could "fix it." He was just a **wedding** guest. What could he do?

At first he was reluctant. More than that, he was rather put out with his mother. I overheard him tell her that it wasn't his time yet. Time for what, I don't know. But his mother just gave him that look—you know the look mother's are so good at.

So Jesus told the servants to fill the ceremonial jars with water. When that was done, he had a servant draw a cup of water from a jar and give it to the wine steward for the **wedding**. Yuck! I certainly hoped he wasn't going to suggest drinking it instead of wine. The hand-washing water? I don't think so! The wine steward lifted the cup to his nose and sniffed and sniffed again. Then he tasted the water. His eyes got big and round. He turned to Jesus. I could tell even then that what he was drinking was not water at all, but the VERY best wine— even better than the wine they had served at the beginning of the **wedding** feast.

Rebekah Ray: Whoa! Water into wine? How did that happen?

Bridesmaid: All I know is that one minute it was water and the next minute it was wine. Jesus did it. Jesus turned the water into wine. If that's not a miracle, I don't know what is.

Rebekah Ray: Wow! What a delicious Bible story.

(Bridesmaid EXITS.)

Rebekah Ray: Now for our final guest and the main course of our delicious Bible stories for today. My producers have told me that we are going to prepare a very special poultry-based salad. I think they got the name wrong. But our next guest can set us straight. It's the Servant Girl from Caiaphas' courtyard.

(Servant Girl ENTERS.)

STORY 5

Servant Girl: Thank you, Rebekah Ray. I'm delighted to be here and share my recipe for Rooster Tabbouleh Salad With Mint.

Rebekah Ray: Rooster Salad? Then my producers got it right. But don't people usually say "chicken salad" instead?

Servant Girl: They might, unless they had been with me in the courtyard at Caiaphas' house. Shall we get started?

(Servant Girl and Rebekah make the Rooster Tabbouleh together.)

Servant Girl: First, we add bulgur wheat that's been soaking in hot water. The soaking makes it tender. Add those chopped tomatoes. Aren't they pretty? So red and ripe and tasty.

Rebekah Ray: Yum, tasty.

Servant Girl: Now put in some of that colorful pepper, the green onions, and the seasonings—mint, parsley, salt, and pepper. Stir it well. Add the olive oil, and drizzle in a little lemon juice. Now it's time for the rooster.

Rebekah Ray: Wherever did you find fresh rooster?

Servant Girl: Oh, I found it one morning in the courtyard. In fact, that's how my story begins. And although we are laughing about adding rooster to the recipe, it was a sad night for all those who followed a man named Jesus. In fact, each time you hear the name **Jesus**, quietly pray, "Lord, forgive us." We will use the customary Hebrew prayer posture each time we say the prayer. Hold your hands upward with palms up and look up.

(As the Servant Girl tells her story, prepare bowls of the Rooster Tabbouleh for the participants.)

Servant Girl: I serve the high priest of the Temple in Jerusalem. His name is Caiaphas. My story begins on the evening of the Passover meal. That night, long after everyone else had gone to bed, there was a great commotion in the courtyard. The Temple guards had arrested a man named **Jesus** and brought him here for trial.

I had heard about **Jesus**. Caiaphas and his group of priests thought he was a troublemaker. They thought he was sure to bring the Romans down on them. But **Jesus** didn't look like that kind of man. And I had heard that he was able to do wonderful things, such as changing water into wine.

Rebekah Ray: Yes, I've heard that rumor too.

Servant Girl: So, while Caiaphas gathered the members of the council together, people began to crowd into the courtyard to see what was going on. As I was standing near the fire, I thought I recognized one of the men. I had seen him with this man **Jesus** before, maybe in the marketplace. I called him out.

But he denied it, saying, "No! I don't know this **Jesus**."

Then several others joined the conversation. They thought they recognized him as well. But each time, the man denied even knowing **Jesus** and moved farther away into the shadows.

Suddenly, everything got quiet. Then the rooster crowed. It was almost morning. The man in question ran from the courtyard. He looked as if he had lost his best friend.

Rebekah Ray: That's a very moving story. Did you ever find out what happened to the man, **Jesus**?

Servant Girl: Yes, but that's another story.

Rebekah Ray: Unfortunately, we are out of time for today. Let's close our meal with the final hand washing. When everyone is finished, we'll say our closing blessing together.

(Have the guests wash their hands and then recite the Closing Blessing.)

We give you thanks, O Lord, for the land you have given us, which has brought forth the food that we have just eaten. Amen.

Rebekah Ray: Tune in tomorrow as we continue our delicious Bible stories. Our guest will be Mary Magdalene, a dear close friend of the man Jesus. She will be sharing her very special bread recipe, Resurrection Rolls.

This is Rebekah Ray wishing you your own delicious encounters with the Bible stories.

People [PEE-puhl] and Places [PLAY-sez]

Abraham [AY-bruh-ham]—The first patriarch. His name was originally Abram, but was changed to Abraham, meaning "father of a multitude." God called Abraham to leave his home and go the land that God would show him.

Sarah [SAIR-uh]—Wife of Abraham. Originally her name was Sarai, but it was changed at the time of the covenant to Sarah. Sarah gave birth to Isaac when she was 91 years old.

Isaac [EYE-zik]—Son of Abraham and Sarah. His name means "he laughs." Isaac is best known for producing twin sons, Jacob and Esau.

Abigail [AB-uh-gayl]—Wife of Nabal and then David's second wife. Abigail intervened between her husband and David and prevented a war.

David [DAY-vid]—The shepherd who was anointed by Samuel to be king after Saul. He is considered Israel's greatest king.

Nabal [NAY-buhl]—A wealthy sheep farmer. His name means "fool." He was married to Abigail and, after the incident with David, died of heart failure.

Esther [ES-tuhr]—Second wife of King Ahasuerus. Esther is known for risking her own life to save the Jews in exile in Persia.

Ahasuerus [uh-has-yoo-ER-uhs]—King of Persia, who ruled over a kingdom that stretched from India to Ethiopia to the Mediterranean Sea. His palaces were opulent.

Mordecai [MOR-duh-kiy]—Esther's cousin. He raised the orphaned Esther and was a Jew who became an official in the court of the King of Persia. Mordecai encouraged his niece to intercede with the king on behalf of the Jews in Persia.

Haman [HAY-muhn]—An official in King Ahasuerus' court. He disliked Jews and plotted to have them exterminated. His plans were thwarted by Queen Esther.

Cana [KAY-nuh]—A village of Galilee, not far from Nazareth. It was the home of Nathanael, one of the disciples.

Caiaphas [KAY-uh-fuhs]—A high priest in Jerusalem. When Jesus was arrested, Jesus was brought to trial in front of him.

Classic Hummus

2 15 oz. cans chickpeas, drained (save water)	½ cup water (from chickpeas)
	salt
2 large cloves garlic, minced	1–2 tbsp. olive oil
¼ cup tahini (sesame paste)	paprika
⅛ cup lemon juice	parsley (for garnish)
1 tsp. ground cumin	

Mash chickpeas with the rock until smooth. Add garlic, tahini, lemon juice, cumin, and ¼ cup water. Puree. Season with salt to taste. Add water until mixture is the consistency of a smooth spread. Spread on paper plate. Drizzle center with olive oil. Sprinkle lightly with paprika and parsley. Serve with pita bread.

GOES WITH STORY 1

Abigail's Date Cakes

1 cup pitted dates	½ cup chopped walnuts
¼ to ½ cup water	¾ cup chopped almonds
1 tsp. cinnamon	honey
¼ tsp. cardamom	

In a blender or food processor, grind the dates to a paste with the water. Add the spices, walnuts, and ¼ cup almonds. Mix well. Form into small balls, coat with honey, and roll in remaining almonds.

GOES WITH STORY 2

Yogurt Sesame Sauce Over Hearts of Palm

1 cup plain yogurt	sprinkle of dill, coriander, parsley
¼ cup tahini (sesame paste)	
1–2 tbsp. lemon juice	1 15 oz. can hearts of palm
salt	

Blend together the yogurt and the tahini. Add the lemon juice. Salt to taste. Season with a sprinkle of the dill, ground coriander, and parsley flakes. Cut hearts of palm into one-inch pieces. Spoon the sauce over each piece.

GOES WITH STORY 3

Cheese Spreads

8 ounces cream cheese

Soften cream cheese. Stir until creamy.

Cinnamon Cheese Spread:

Add 2 teaspoons cinnamon, salt, 1 teaspoon honey.
Stir until well mixed.

Black Cumin Seed Cheese Spread:

Add 1–3 teaspoons black cumin seed.

Add salt to taste and a sprinkle of parsley.

Horseradish Cheese Spread

Add 1 tablespoon horseradish. Salt to taste.

GOES WITH STORY 4

Rooster Tabbouleh Salad With Mint

1 cup fine bulgur wheat	salt
4 plum tomatoes	ground pepper
1 red or yellow pepper,	6–8 tbsp. olive oil
chopped	¼ cup lemon juice
4 green onions	2 ½–3 cups diced grilled
¾ cup finely chopped parsley	chicken
½ cup finely chopped mint	romaine lettuce leaves

Pour hot water over bulgar wheat. Soak it until it is
completely cool and tender. Drain. Dice tomatoes and pepper.

Mix in chopped onions, parsley, mint, and bulgur wheat.

Add salt, pepper, olive oil, lemon juice, and chicken.

Serve with romaine leaves.   GOES WITH STORY 5

Adjusting the Recipes for Your Event

The recipes provided here will easily serve fifty people a "taste." If, however, you are using the table style setup, adjust according to the number of participants you expect.

Two tables with 8 people (16):
Divide the ingredients for each recipe in half. For example, instead of two cans of chickpeas, use one can. Since it is difficult to divide a can of hearts of palm in half, cut bigger pieces. For the rooster salad, cut the recipe in half and serve larger portions.

Four tables with 8 people (32):
You have two choices:
1. Divide each recipe in half, as with the two tables. You will have smaller portion sizes, but that will be O.K.
2. Use the full recipe and provide larger portion sizes.

Six tables with 8 people (48):
Use the recipes as printed. This will provide larger portion sizes and a few "seconds" on those particularly tasty dishes (such as the date cakes and the cheese spread).

The Rooster Tabbouleh Salad With Mint (prepared at the front table) will easily serve the larger number of people. People actually came back for seconds on this one, as it is quite tasty. Cut the recipe in half for the smaller number of participants. You will probably still have leftovers.

Abraham and Sarah	Abigail and David	Queen Esther	A Wedding at Cana

Opening Blessing
Blessed art thou, Jehovah, our God, King of the world, who causes to come forth bread from the earth.
Amen.

Closing Blessing
We give you thanks, O Lord, for the land you have given us, which has brought forth the food that we have just eaten.
Amen.

Bibliography

Daily Life at the Time of Jesus by Miriam Vamosh (Abingdon Press, 2001). ISBN: 0687048915

Feast From the Mideast: 250 Sun-Drenched Dishes From the Lands of the Bible by Faye Levy (HarperCollins, 2003). ISBN: 0060093617

The Good Book Cookbook: Recipes From Biblical Times by Naomi Goodman, Robert Marcus, and Susan Woolhandler (Dodd Mead, 1986). ISBN: 0396085784

How People Lived in the Bible: The Illustrated Guide (Thomas Nelson, 2002). ISBN: 0785242562

The Land & People Jesus Knew by J. Robert Teringo (Bethany House Publishers, 1985) ISBN: 0871237970

Manners and Customs in the Bible by Victor H. Matthews (Hendrickson Publishers, 2006). ISBN: 9781598560596

Manners and Customs of Bible Lands by Fred H. Wight (Moody Press, 1983). ISBN: 0824041636

DELICIOUS BIBLE STORIES

Everyone loves a good story, and everyone loves to eat. *Delicious Bible Stories* combines the two with fun and exciting results. Participants are invited to be a part of a popular "cooking show" as various "guests" from the Bible come to share their stories and their delicious recipes.

This resource not only presents authentic Bible-times recipes, but it also introduces customs and actions to make it even more participatory.

From the tale of Sarah's famous laugh to the account of what happened the night Jesus was tried before council, participants will immerse themselves in the story in a totally experiential way.

Delicious Bible Stories provides detailed instruction on how to set up the event in a variety of ways—around tables with everyone involved with the preparation, as a sampling experience that will give one hundred people a "taste" of the Bible, or as five separate sessions.

Some of recipes included are Sarah's Homemade Hummus, Abigail's Famous Date Cakes, Esther's Hearts of Palm (straight from Babylonia), and the classic Rooster Tabbouleh. (So that's what happened to that rooster!)

Delicious Bible Stories includes ingredient lists tips for each dish. Two scripts are included so t choose whichever model suits their church situa

Delicious Bible Stories gives everyone who partici event a chance to understand Bible culture just a li

Abingdon Press
gdonpress.com

design by Paige Easter

ISBN-13: 978-1-4267-0032-3

90000

9 781426 700323

MOON DOGS SERIES

NED, THE CAT

Story by Tamar Reis-Frankfort and Clair Baker
Illustrated by Asha and Drew Wilson
Edited by Wendy Tweedie

Encourage the reader to read the words by blending the sounds together from left to right throughout the word.

There are some common words in this book that the reader may need help with at this stage. These words may contain new sounds or complex spellings: has, a, off, the, is

Check the reader knows the target sounds in this book and their corresponding letters.

d e f v

FIRS ESTATE PRIMARY SCHOOL